GEORGE Washington

GEORGE
Washington
A PICTURE BOOK BIOGRAPHY

by James Cross Giblin
Illustrated by Michael Dooling

SCHOLASTIC INC.
New York Toronto London Auckland Sydney

ACKNOWLEDGMENTS

The following books were especially helpful in the researching of this book:

George Washington by John R. Alden. Baton Rouge: The Louisiana State University Press, 1984

George Washington: Man and Monument by Marcus Cunliffe. Boston: Little, Brown & Company, 1958

George Washington: A Biography by Washington Irving. Abridged and edited with an introduction by Charles Neider. Garden City, New York: Doubleday & Company, Inc., 1976

The Life and Memorable Actions of George Washington by Mason Locke Weems, edited by Marcus Cunliffe. Cambridge, Massachusetts: The Belknap Press, Harvard, 1962

Rules of Civility and Decent Behavior in Company and Conversation by George Washington. Boston: Applewood Books, 1988

Washington: The Indispensable Man by James Thomas Flexner. Boston: Little, Brown & Company, 1969

The author is also indebted to Mary Downing Hahn, who drove him to Mount Vernon, and to the guides there, who provided valuable insights into the lives of George and Martha Washington, and the members of their household.

ISBN 0-590-48101-0

Title calligraphy by Jeanyee Wong. Map calligraphy by Jerry Kelly.
Book design by Claire Counihan.
Michael Dooling's artwork is done in oil paint on canvas.

FOR
Dianne Hess
— J.C.G.

FOR
Jane
— M.D.

GEORGE WASHINGTON grew up in a big family. His father had been married before, and George had two older half brothers, Lawrence and Augustine. He also had three younger brothers, Samuel, John, and Charles, and a younger sister, Elizabeth. They all lived and worked and played on a farm in Virginia called Ferry Farm.

George was an athletic boy, and tall for his age. His father gave him a pony and taught him how to ride.

Mr. Washington sent George's half brothers to the same school he had gone to in England. But George went to school near home. There a minister taught him how to read and write and do sums. George had a hard time with spelling. Was it *coff* or *cough*?

Nothing really bad happened to George until he was eleven. That was when his father died.

Now George looked to his half brother, Lawrence, for guidance. Lawrence taught him how to hunt and to shoot. George became a very good marksman.

George yearned for adventure and wanted to go to sea as a sailor. But his mother wouldn't let him, so George stayed in school.

Lawrence married and moved to a farm called Mount Vernon. His house stood on a hill that sloped down to the Potomac River.

George often visited his brother at Mount Vernon, and he came to love the place. Some days he and Lawrence went fishing in the river. Other days they went fox hunting with Lawrence's hounds.

When he was just sixteen, George got the chance to help survey land on Virginia's western frontier. He had a fine time on the trip. Besides measuring land, he swam horses across flooded rivers. He watched Indians perform a war dance. He roasted wild turkeys over open fires and slept under the stars.

Back home, a new tragedy struck. Lawrence fell ill with tuberculosis and died a year later. First George had lost his father. Now he had lost his beloved half brother. At age twenty, he was on his own.

America was still a colony at that time. That meant it was ruled by its parent country, Great Britain. The British army defended America's western frontier. Helping the army were groups of volunteer soldiers called militias. George joined the Virginia militia as a major.

George and his men marched with the British into the forests and mountains of the Ohio country. Both Great Britain and France claimed this wilderness was theirs.

George fought back bravely when the French attacked. Two horses were shot out from under him. Bullets ripped through his uniform. His commanding officer was killed. But George wasn't even wounded.

At last the French gave up. American settlers began to move into the Ohio country. His work done, George put away his uniform. He went back to Mount Vernon and became a farmer.

Every well-to-do farmer in Virginia owned slaves then. With the help of his slaves, George raised crops of tobacco, wheat, and Indian corn.

Now that he had settled down, George decided to look for a wife. He found a pretty young widow, Martha Custis. Martha had two small children— John, who was called Jackie, and Martha, who was called Patsy. Martha also owned 100 slaves.

Martha and the children and the slaves all came to live at Mount Vernon. George added rooms to the house and built new cabins for the slave families.

George and Martha had no children of their own, but George doted on Jackie and Patsy. He ordered books and toys for them from faraway London.

Life rolled along happily for many years. Then Patsy got sick. She suffered from epilepsy and had seizures. Her mother and George took Patsy from doctor to doctor, but nothing helped. Patsy died when she was only seventeen.

George was still grieving for Patsy when he got a new call to duty.

Many Americans wanted to be free of Great Britain. They wanted to be independent, and run their own country. Things got so tense that fighting broke out between British troops and American volunteers. It happened at the little towns of Lexington and Concord in Massachusetts.

America had never had a Commander in Chief of its armed forces. Now Congress decided it needed one. The members talked and talked and finally made their choice. They all agreed that the best man for the job would be George Washington.

George wasn't sure he could do it. And he hated to leave Mount Vernon. But he believed in American independence and wanted to help win it. So at last he said yes. But he would not accept any pay, only his expenses.

The fighting went well at first. George's men drove the British out of Boston. Then they moved south to build defenses around New York. Congress declared America's independence from Great Britain.

But then the British sent a large army to attack New York. They forced George and his men to give up the city and cross the Hudson River into New Jersey.

George rallied his army by planning a surprise attack on the British forces. Hidden by darkness, he led his men in boats across the icy Delaware River. At dawn on Christmas Day, they attacked the enemy camp at Trenton, New Jersey. Most of the soldiers in the camp were still asleep, and they surrendered quickly.

George won another battle at Princeton, but then he lost one near Philadelphia the following fall. With his men, he had to retreat to Valley Forge, Pennsylvania.

It was bitterly cold at Valley Forge. George lived in a stone house, but his soldiers had to sleep in tents until they could build log huts. The soldiers did not have enough food or clothing or shoes. When they went from tent to tent, they left bloody footprints in the snow.

George wrote to Congress and begged for more supplies. But the supplies were slow to come. When they did, George made sure every man got an equal share of clothing. He made sure the food was divided equally, too. At last the long winter ended. The American army had survived. And new help was on the way.

France recognized America as an independent nation. It sent troops to fight alongside the American soldiers.

George and his men were filled with fresh hope. But the war was far from over. The Americans and their French allies won some battles, but they lost many others. The soldiers still did not have enough to eat or to wear. Some of them ran away from the army and went back home.

George often wished he could go home to Mount Vernon. But he knew he could never leave his men. Nor could he give up the struggle for America's independence. So he stayed. And, seeing his determination, most of his men stayed with him.

At last came the opportunity George had been waiting for.

A large British force was camped at Yorktown, Virginia. George and his men surrounded the British by land. A fleet of French ships blocked their escape by sea. With no hope of help, the British surrendered to George. He took more than 7000 prisoners.

Yorktown was the greatest victory the American army had won. But George's joy about it soon turned to sadness.

Martha's son, Jackie, was with the army at Yorktown. Just before the victory, he came down with a high fever, and soon afterward he died. George brought his body back to Mount Vernon for burial.

23

A year and a half after Yorktown, the American Revolutionary War finally came to an end. Under General George Washington's leadership, the United States had won its freedom. No man in America was more loved than he. Many people even said that he should become King of the United States.

George would not hear of it. He hadn't fought for America's freedom against the King of England only to be crowned king himself. All he wanted, he said, was to retire to Mount Vernon. And after saying farewell to his officers, that is what he did.

George loved being a farmer again. He got up at dawn and ate a breakfast of hoecakes and tea. Then he rode from field to field to see what the work gangs were doing.

25

He and Martha were never alone. Relatives and friends often filled every spare bedroom. And after Jackie's death, the Washingtons took in Jackie's two youngest children, George and Nelly. Every day Nelly practiced on the harpsichord in the little parlor. George liked to sit and listen to her play.

But these happy days did not last long. Soon George got another call to duty—a call he could not refuse.

Delegates from twelve of the thirteen states met in Philadelphia to write a new plan, a constitution, for the government of the United States. The Constitution said the country should have a strong president, who would be elected for a term of four years.

Electors in each state cast ballots for America's first President. When the ballots were counted, no one was surprised at the result. All of the electors had voted for George Washington.

So once again George packed his bags and set off by himself. He traveled by carriage to New York City, which was then the capital of the United States.

Crowds in every town and village cheered George as his carriage passed by. He waved back and smiled, but behind the smile he was nervous. What would it be like to be President of the United States? No one had ever been President before.

When he took the oath of office, George did not wear his general's uniform or a fancy outfit made in England or France. Instead he wore a plain brown suit made in America. That way, no one would think he wanted to be king.

Still, some people wanted to call George "His Highness." He said he preferred "Mr. President." And that is what America's Presidents have been called ever since.

Martha joined George in New York and took up her duties as America's first First Lady. A year later, the capital of the United States was moved to Philadelphia. George and Martha moved, too.

George discovered that it was as hard being President as it was being Commander in Chief of the Army. Maybe harder. Some people believed the central government should be strong. It should start a national bank and raise new taxes. Other people feared this would lead to a government like Great Britain's. They wanted the states to have more power.

George listened to both sides. He thought carefully. Then he made his decisions. Usually he decided in favor of a stronger central government.

When his four-year term ended, George wanted to retire to Mount Vernon. But the other government leaders told him he could not. They said George was the only man who could keep the country together and lead it forward. So he ran again. And he was elected again.

New troubles came in George's second term. The French overthrew their king and announced that France was now a republic. Soon afterward, they went to war with Great Britain.

Some Americans thought the United States should take France's side. Hadn't the French helped us win the American Revolution? And hadn't Great Britain been our enemy?

Other Americans thought the United States should not take any side. America was still a new, young nation. It had neither a strong army nor a strong navy. If it got into a war, it might lose its independence.

As always, George listened to both sides. He thought carefully. And then he made his decision. The United States would not take any side.

George was over sixty years old now, and he felt his age. He feared that his memory was failing. And his false teeth bothered him. They were made from the teeth of a hippopotamus, and did not fit well.

George was wearing his false teeth when he had his portrait painted by Gilbert Stuart. This is the picture of him that appears on every dollar bill. George looks very serious in the picture because his teeth were hurting him that day.

George's second term was coming to an end. He could look back with pride on his years as President. Great Britain had left the Ohio country, and more and more settlers were moving into it. American ships now sailed up and down the Mississippi River. Three new states, Vermont, Kentucky, and Tennessee, had joined the United States. The new capital city, Washington, named for George, was being laid out along the Potomac River.

Many people wanted George to run for a third term, but he refused. He said the time had come to retire for good. And he meant it.

George was happy to be home at Mount Vernon. Once more he got up at dawn and ate a breakfast of hoecakes and tea. Then he rode from field to field to see what the work gangs were doing. But something was troubling him.

During his years in the North, George had seen a world without slaves. Now he was back in the South, where slaves did most of the work on farms like Mount Vernon. Was it right? George wondered. Should slavery be allowed in a free country like the United States? He decided it should not.

George knew his Southern neighbors would not agree with his ideas about slavery. But he could do something about it on his own. In his will, he said that after his death, and Martha's, all the slaves at Mount Vernon were to be freed.

One day in December, George rode out in a freezing rain to inspect his fields as usual. The next day he came down with a sore throat. The day after that his throat was so swollen that he could not swallow. Breathing was difficult and he could barely speak.

Doctors were called, but in those days there were no medicines that could cure George. "I am not afraid to go," he whispered to Martha. And that night, near midnight, he died.

George Washington left behind no children of his own. Instead he left a nation. A nation that he had served as its first Commander in Chief, and then as its first President. That is why he is known as "The Father of His Country."

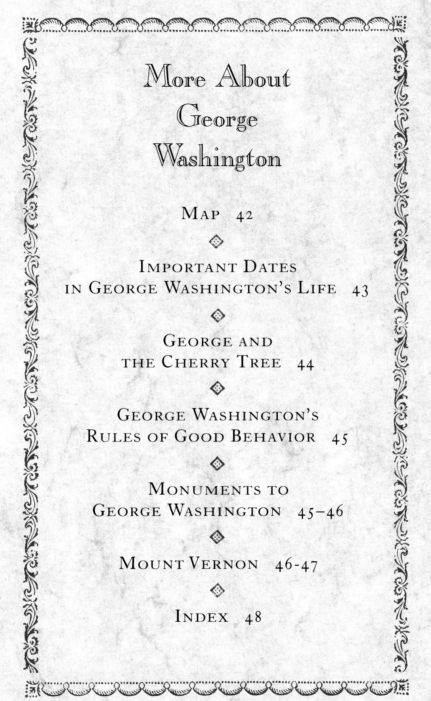

More About George Washington

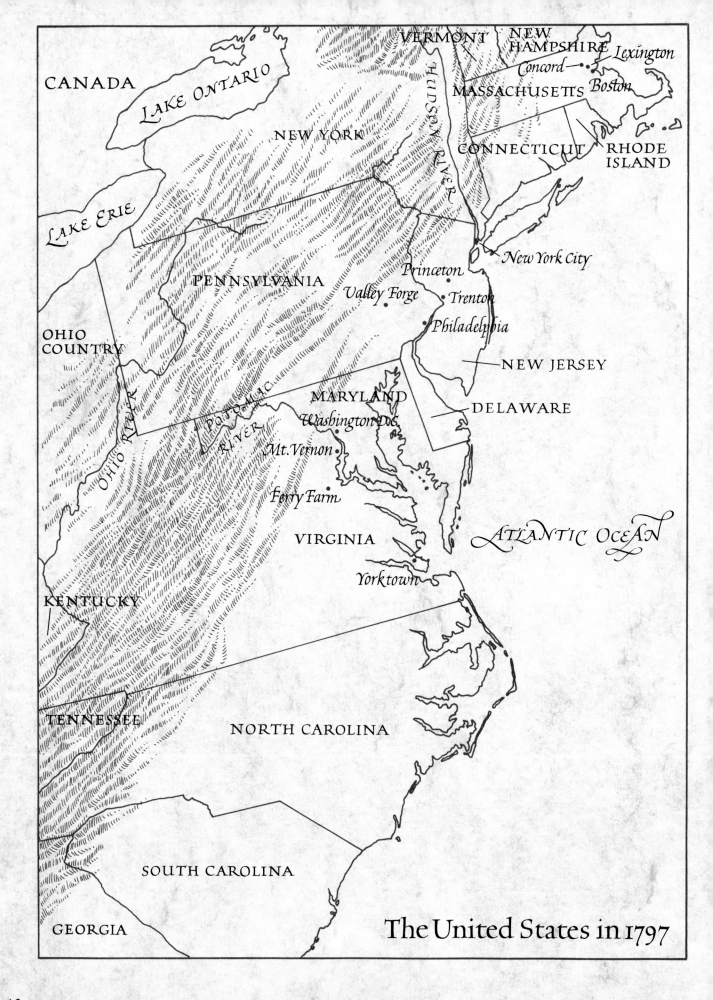

CANADA

LAKE ONTARIO

LAKE ERIE

VERMONT

NEW HAMPSHIRE

Concord — *Lexington*

Boston

MASSACHUSETTS

NEW YORK

Hudson River

CONNECTICUT

RHODE ISLAND

PENNSYLVANIA

New York City

Princeton

Valley Forge — *Trenton*

Philadelphia

OHIO COUNTRY

NEW JERSEY

Potomac River

MARYLAND

DELAWARE

Ohio River

Washington D.C.

Mt. Vernon

Ferry Farm

ATLANTIC OCEAN

VIRGINIA

Yorktown

KENTUCKY

NORTH CAROLINA

TENNESSEE

SOUTH CAROLINA

GEORGIA

The United States in 1797

IMPORTANT DATES IN GEORGE WASHINGTON'S LIFE

February 11, 1732 — George is born on a farm in Virginia. (In 1752, eleven more days were added to the calendar. After that, George's birthday was celebrated on February 22.)

April 12, 1743 — George's father, Augustine Washington, dies.

July 26, 1752 — George's half brother, Lawrence, dies.

November 6, 1752 — George is appointed a major in the Virginia militia.

January 6, 1759 — George marries Mrs. Martha Custis.

April 19, 1775 — The American Revolutionary War begins with an armed clash between British and American forces at Lexington and Concord, Massachusetts.

June 16, 1775 — George is elected General and Commander in Chief of the Continental (American) army.

July 4, 1776 — The Second Continental Congress adopts the Declaration of Independence.

December 25–26, 1776 — George and his men cross the Delaware River and defeat the British forces at Trenton, New Jersey.

The winter of 1777–1778 — George and his men suffer at Valley Forge.

October 19, 1781 — The British surrender at Yorktown, Virginia.

April 18, 1783 — The fighting in the American Revolutionary War ends.

February 4, 1789 — George is elected President of the United States.

December 5, 1792 — George is reelected for a second term as President.

March 1797 — George retires as President and goes home to Mount Vernon.

December 14, 1799 — George Washington dies at Mount Vernon.

George and the Cherry Tree

When we hear the name George Washington, one of the first things we usually think of is the story of George and the cherry tree. But we may not know the whole story, or where it came from.

The story first appeared in a book for young readers called *The Life and Memorable Actions of George Washington*, written by Mason Locke Weems. The book was published in 1800, just a year after George Washington's death. Weems said his purpose in writing it was "to inspire patriotic devotion and high moral standards in the youth of the country."

Weems claimed the story was told to him by an old lady who was a distant relative of the Washington family. As a girl, she had often visited the Washingtons at Ferry Farm. It was there that she heard the story.

"When George was about six years old, he was made the master of a little hatchet," the old lady told Weems. "After that he went about chopping everything that came in his way.

"One day in the garden, where George often amused himself by hacking his mother's pea-sticks, he tried the edge of his hatchet on the trunk of a beautiful, young English cherry tree. He barked it so terribly that I don't believe the tree ever got over it."

The old lady went on to tell what happened when George's father found out about the tree. Furious, he demanded to know who had hacked it. Just then George entered the room with his little hatchet.

"George," said his father, "do you know who killed that beautiful young cherry tree yonder in the garden?"

In the old lady's words, George "staggered under the question for a moment, then looked at his father. 'I can't tell a lie, Pa,' he bravely cried out. 'You know I can't tell a lie. I did cut it with my hatchet.'

"'Run to my arms, you dearest boy,' cried his father in return, 'run to my arms. Glad am I, George, that you killed my tree, for you have paid me for it a thousandfold by telling the truth.'"

The story of George and the cherry tree was extremely popular. It was told and retold in many different versions, and was included in McGuffey's *Eclectic Readers* that every school child read in the mid and late 1800s.

Is the story true? From all the evidence we have, no, it is not. And the old lady who supposedly told it to Mason Locke Weems probably wasn't a real person, either.

In Weems's time, writers often made up stories about famous people in order to prove a point, such as George Washington's honesty. Their readers didn't seem to mind. They enjoyed a story like the one about George and the cherry tree for its own sake. And so can we — as long as we don't make the mistake of thinking it really happened.

GEORGE WASHINGTON'S RULES OF GOOD BEHAVIOR

When George Washington was 14 years old, he copied a list of 110 rules of good behavior for a school assignment. They came from the English translation of a French book on manners. Although the rules were not original with George, he — like other young men of his time — tried to live by them. Here is a sampling of the rules:

1. Sleep not when others speak, sit not when others stand, speak not when you should hold your peace, walk not on when others stop.

2. Do not laugh too much or too loud in public.

3. Wear not your clothes foul, ripped, or dusty, but see that they be brushed once every day, at least.

4. Being set at a meal, scratch not; neither spit, cough, nor blow your nose, except if there is a necessity for it.

5. Think before you speak; pronounce not imperfectly nor bring out your words too hastily, but orderly and distinctly.

6. Undertake not what you cannot perform, but be careful to keep your promise.

MONUMENTS TO GEORGE WASHINGTON

Besides our national capital, 121 other American towns and villages have been named for George Washington. So have 1 American state, 7 mountains, 10 lakes, 33 counties, and 9 colleges and universities.

George's face appears on coins and one-dollar bills and postage stamps. His portrait hangs in countless offices and classrooms. There are statues of him all over the United States and the world. His head — 60 feet from top to bottom — has been carved out of the side of Mount Rushmore in South Dakota.

But probably the most famous tribute to George Washington is the Washington

Monument in Washington, D.C. A monument is something set up to help keep alive the memory of a person or an event.

Congress first talked about building a monument to George in 1783, while he was President. But because of difficulties in raising money, construction of the monument didn't start until July 4, 1848. The Civil War of 1861–1865 delayed it further, and the monument wasn't completed until 1884. It finally opened to the public on October 9, 1888, almost 90 years after George Washington's death.

In shape, the monument is what is called an *obelisk*. It is a four-sided stone pillar that tapers toward a pyramid at the top. The width of the monument at the base is 55 feet, while the width at the top is only 34 feet. The monument is 555 feet high, which makes it the tallest structure in the city of Washington.

The top may be reached by elevator or by an iron stairway of 897 steps. Most visitors to the monument take the elevator. It rises from the bottom to the top in just 70 seconds.

Thousands of tourists come to the Washington Monument each year. From the observation deck, they have wonderful views of the city in every direction. And if they follow the winding path of the Potomac River to the southeast, they can see almost as far as Mount Vernon.

MOUNT VERNON

After George Washington's death, Martha Washington lived on at Mount Vernon until her death on May 22, 1802. Then the last of the slaves at Mount Vernon were freed, as George had specified in his will.

George's nephew, Bushrod Washington, inherited Mount Vernon. By 1850 Bushrod, too, was dead, and Mount Vernon belonged to his great-nephew, John Augustine Washington, Jr.

No matter how hard he worked, John Augustine could not make a profit from Mount Vernon. As a result, the mansion became run-down. Paint was peeling from the walls, the roof leaked, and chunks of plaster had fallen from the ceiling. John Augustine tried to sell the estate to both the state of Virginia and the federal government, but neither of them wanted it.

The mansion was in danger of being torn down when a woman from South Carolina, Ann Pamela Cunningham, came to its rescue. She organized the Mount Vernon Ladies' Association, and the association launched a nationwide campaign to raise funds. By 1858 they had gathered $200,000. With that amount, the association was able to buy the mansion house at Mount Vernon and two hundred acres of land around it.

The association restored the house and grounds, and opened them to the public. During the Civil War, Mount Vernon was declared off-limits to the fighting. Both Union soldiers from the North and Confederate soldiers from the South wanted to see the home of George Washington, but they had to leave their guns at the gate.

The association needed funds for the upkeep of the mansion and grounds, so it charged the soldiers 25¢ each to tour Mount Vernon. That policy continues to this day. The association, which still maintains Mount Vernon, charges every visitor an admission fee. It receives no funds from the federal or the state governments.

Today, Mount Vernon is the most visited historic home in the United States. More than one million people tour the mansion and grounds each year. In the mansion, the visitors can stroll through the rooms in which the Washingtons lived and worked. The rooms are painted in bright shades of green and Prussian blue as they were in the Washingtons' day.

In the little parlor, the visitors can see the harpsichord on which Martha's grand-daughter, Nelly Custis, played. Farther on, they can walk through George's study. In this room are the desk and upholstered swivel chair that he used when he was President. A portrait of his beloved half brother, Lawrence, hangs on the wall.

Upstairs, the visitors can look into the master bedroom where George Washington died. George was six feet, two inches tall in a time when most men were only about five feet seven. So Martha had a bed specially made for him in Philadelphia. It is six-and-a-half feet long and six feet wide.

To the southwest of the mansion, halfway down a gentle slope, the visitors will find the red-brick tomb of George and Martha Washington. Above the entrance to the tomb is a stone tablet. The inscription on it says: "Within this Enclosure Rest the remains of Gen. George Washington." Behind the iron gate to the tomb are two marble coffins. One is inscribed simply "Washington." The other is inscribed "Martha, consort [wife] to Washington."

Every year, on Washington's birthday, a special group of visitors comes to Mount Vernon. They are the descendants of George's three brothers and his sister. After gathering at the mansion house, these men and women from all over the country walk down to the tomb. There they bow their heads and lay a wreath on the coffin of George Washington.

INDEX

Page numbers in italic indicate illustrations.